Many different horses and
ponies are looking forward to
be discovered and colored!

We hope you have lots of fun
coloring and doodling :-)

_____

Name of the artist

We hope you liked this book!

It would mean a lot to us to receive feedback, praise or criticism in form of a rating on Amazon or via e-mail at booksbykwabu@gmail.com.

THANK YOU!
:-)

ISBN: 979-8569759453

Imprint:

Kwabu LLC

Attn: Wes Holmstrom

PO Box 1023

Refugio, TX 78377

Made in the USA
Las Vegas, NV
26 October 2023